# DISCOVER DOGS WITH
## THE AMERICAN CANINE ASSOCIATION

AMERICAN CANINE ASSOCIATION, INC.

ACA

America's Largest Veterinary Health Tracking Canine Registry

OFFICIAL SEAL ®

## ♥ ♥ ♥ ♥ ♥ I LIKE ♥ ♥ ♥ ♥ ♥
# BEAGLES!

Linda Bozzo

It is the Mission of the American Canine Association (ACA) to provide registered dog owners with the educational support needed for raising, training, showing, and breeding the healthiest pets expected by responsible pet owners throughout the world. Through our activities and services, we encourage and support the dog world in order to promote best-known husbandry standards as well as to ensure that the voice and needs of our customers are quickly and properly addressed.

Our continued support, commitment, and direction are guided by our customers, including veterinary, legal, and legislative advisors. ACA aims to provide the most efficient, cooperative, and courteous service to our customers and strives to set the standard for education and problem solving for all who depend on our services.

For more information, please visit www.acacanines.com, e-mail customerservice@acadogs.com, phone 1-800-651-8332, or write to the American Canine Association at PO Box 121107, Clermont, FL 34712.

Enslow Elementary, an imprint of Enslow Publishers, Inc.

Enslow Elementary® is a registered trademark of Enslow Publishers, Inc.

**Library of Congress Cataloging-in-Publication Data**

Bozzo, Linda.
   I like beagles! / Linda Bozzo.
       p. cm. — (Discover dogs with the american canine association)
   Includes bibliographical references and index.
   Summary: "Early readers will learn how to care for a beagle, including breed-specific traits and needs"—Provided by publisher.
   ISBN 978-0-7660-3846-2
   1.  Beagle (Dog breed)—Juvenile literature.  I. Title.
SF429.B3B69 2012
636.753'7—dc22
                              2011010473

Future editions:
Paperback ISBN 978-1-4644-0123-7
ePUB ISBN 978-1-4645-1030-4
PDF ISBN 978-1-4646-1030-1

Printed in China

012012 Leo Paper Group, Heshan City, Guangdong, China

10 9 8 7 6 5 4 3 2 1

**To Our Readers:** We have done our best to make sure all Internet Addresses in this book were active and appropriate when we went to press. However, the author and the publisher have no control over and assume no liability for the material available on those Internet sites or on other Web sites they may link to. Any comments or suggestions can be sent by e-mail to comments@enslow.com or to the address on the back cover.

Every effort has been made to locate all copyright holders of material used in this book. If any errors or omissions have occurred, corrections will be made in future editions of this book.

**Photo Credits:** Angelika Fischer/Photos.com, p. 13 (hamburger); Annette Shaff/Photos.com, p. 13 (collar); Image Source/Photolibrary, p. 8; © iStockphoto.com/Willie B. Thomas, p. 18; jclegg/Photos.com, p. 13 (leash and rope); © Jeff Greenberg/Alamy, p. 21; © Myrleen Pearson/PhotoEdit Inc., pp. 5, 9; Shutterstock.com, pp. 1, 3, 4, 6, 10, 11, 13 (beagle, bed, brush, bowls), 14, 17, 22, 23.

**Cover Photo:** Shutterstock.com (beagle puppy).

**Enslow Elementary**
an imprint of
**Enslow Publishers, Inc.**
40 Industrial Road
Box 398
Berkeley Heights, NJ 07922
USA

http://www.enslow.com

# CONTENTS

# IS A BEAGLE RIGHT FOR YOU?

Beagles are gentle, friendly dogs that love being around people and other dogs. They are great family pets.

**FUN FACT:**
Beagles bay when they are excited. Baying is a cross between barking and howling.

Beagles love to be with their families.

A puppy needs more attention than an older dog.

# A DOG OR PUPPY?

Puppies are fun to play with. But a young beagle can be hard to train. She would need a lot of attention.

If you do not have time to train a puppy, an older beagle that is already trained may be better for you.

Beagles will grow to be small to medium in size.

# LOVING YOUR BEAGLE

Your beagle will need love.
Spend time with him.
Pet, play, and talk to
your dog. Beagles have
loads of love to share!

Show your beagle love, and he will love you right back!

You can play a Frisbee® game with your beagle!

# EXERCISE

Beagles need lots of exercise. You will want to walk your beagle often using a leash. Beagles love to play games, like **fetch**.

Tugging on a rope is also fun!

# FEEDING YOUR BEAGLE

Beagles can be fed wet or dry dog food. Ask a **veterinarian (vet)**, a doctor for animals, which food to feed your dog and how much to feed her. Give your beagle fresh, clean water every day.

Remember to keep your dog's food and water dishes clean. Dirty dishes can make her sick.

Do not feed your beagle people food. It can make her sick.

## Your new dog will need:

a collar with a tag

a bed

a brush

food and water dishes

a leash

toys

Be careful not to get water inside your beagle's ears! It could give her an earache!

# GROOMING

Beagles have short hair. They only need to be brushed once or twice a week. A beagle's ears should be cleaned often by an adult.

Your dog should be bathed about every six to eight weeks. Use a gentle soap made just for dogs when bathing your beagle.

You also need to clip your dog's nails. A vet or **groomer** can show you how.

# WHAT YOU SHOULD KNOW

Beagles do not like to be bothered when they eat. They like to bark and howl. These dogs like to chew things.

Beagles also enjoy hunting. They are very good at following scents, or smells. Beagles were born to track animals. Be careful not to let your beagle wander off by himself. He could get lost.

Get your beagle some chew toys to play with.

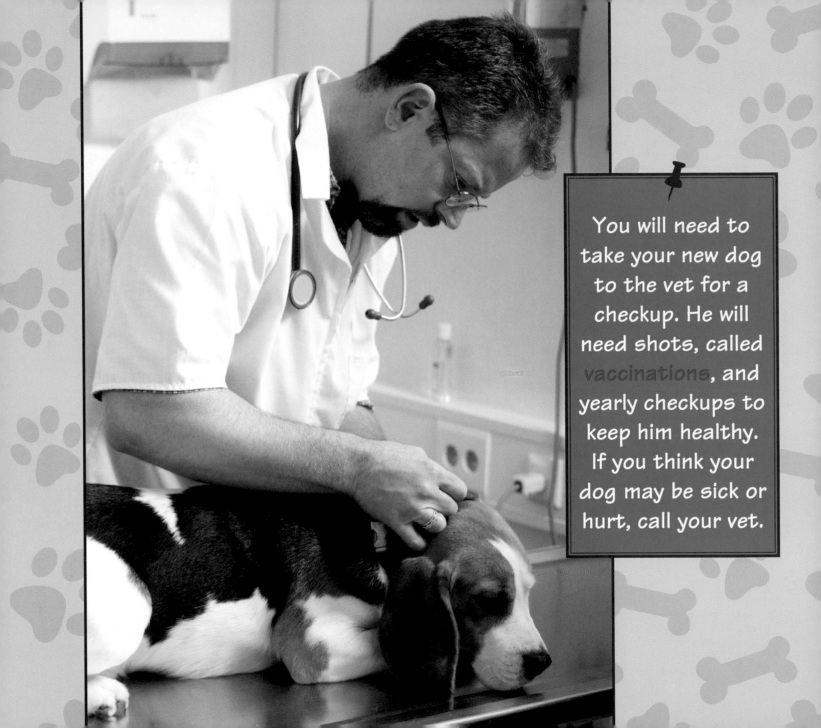

You will need to take your new dog to the vet for a checkup. He will need shots, called vaccinations, and yearly checkups to keep him healthy. If you think your dog may be sick or hurt, call your vet.

# A GOOD FRIEND

Beagles can live up to ten to fifteen years. During that time, your beagle will need you to keep him healthy and happy.

Your beagle will be a good friend. Love and care for your beagle, and he will be a terrific pet for many years!

# NOTE TO PARENTS

It is important to consider having your dog spayed or neutered when the dog is young. Spaying and neutering are operations that prevent unwanted puppies and can help improve the overall health of your dog.

It is also a good idea to microchip your dog, in case he or she gets lost. A vet will implant a microchip under the skin that contains your contact information, which can then be scanned at a vet's office or animal shelter.

Some towns require licenses for dogs, so be sure to check with your town clerk.

For more information, speak with a vet.

There are many dogs, young and old, waiting to be adopted from animal shelters and rescue groups.

**bay**—To make a sound that is between a bark and a howl.

**fetch**—To go after a toy and bring it back.

**groomer**—A person who cuts a dog's fur and nails.

**vaccinations**—Shots that dogs need to stay healthy.

**veterinarian (vet)**—A doctor for animals.

## Books

Beal, Abigail. *I Love My Beagle.* New York: PowerKids Press, 2011.

Gagne, Tammy. *Beagles.* Mankato, Minn.: Capstone Press, 2010.

Landau, Elaine. *Beagles Are the Best!* Minneapolis, Minn.: Lerner Publications, 2010.

## Internet Addresses

**American Canine Association: Kids Corner**
<http://acakids.com/>

**Janet Wall's How to Love Your Dog: The Beagle**
<http://loveyourdog.com/beagles.html>

# INDEX